A Universal Children's Book
(and for those who read it to them)

WILLIAM R. MRAZEK

outskirtspress
DENVER, COLORADO

This book is dedicated to my beautiful wife Gloria, who always supports and encourages me in everything I do, to our wonderful children Danielle (Dani) and Bill(y), who have always been and continue to be the most blessed gift a couple could receive, and to my dad William C. Mrazek, who taught me the meaning of 'acceptance', not just with words, but by continuous example.

I love you all.

I would like to thank everyone at Outskirts Press for all of their help, advice, and encouragement with this book. It is my first Children's book, and they made the publishing process much easier than I ever would have anticipated. I specifically would like to acknowledge Jerry Banks, Colleen Goulet, Cheri Breeding Miller, Elaine Simpson, and an extra special thank you, thank you, thank you to a wonderful and creative artist and illustrator who brought life to WE with her terrific illustrations, Ginger Triplett. Thank you all very, very much!

An Introduction to "WE"
by
William R. Mrazek

There are many people who influence us when we are children; parents, grandparents, brothers & sisters, aunts & uncles, cousins, teachers, friends, guardians, baby sitters, day care personnel, and playmates. We are cared for, fed, clothed, protected, educated, and guided in how we think, speak, feel, act, and react to those around us throughout life. As children, we rely on and learn from those who provide and care for us. It is during this formative time that the foundation is established for our thoughts, opinions, fears, self-confidence, self-doubt, strengths and weaknesses, and ultimately, our actions toward our self and each other.

I wrote this children's book, entitled "WE", because I believe that we can guide children early on in life that it is OK and normal that we are all different, and provide it in a simple, fun to read rhyme style verse that will be memorable and lasting, like a song verse. It is important that the children associate the verses with illustrations that are recognizable; not cartoonish or distorted. Therefore, the illustrations in the book were purposely designed to be soft and colorful, visually and mentally stimulating, and realistic so that when children do see an adult or child with a characteristic represented in the book, they can identify it with the illustration and not view the person as someone who is strange, inferior, or the subject of ridicule. "WE" will also help children raise their own level of self-confidence when they see some of their own characteristics illustrated in the book. I believe that raising and improving a child's self-confidence, as well as their perception of others, is a key factor in helping to diminish bullying during childhood, and possibly more serious acts of violence later in life.

A term that has been used to help address the issue of racism, bigotry, bullying, and general negative perception-based actions toward each other, is "Tolerance". The movement for tolerance is a noble one and certainly is deserving of merit in its endeavor. It is an excellent introduction to change, and quite possibly a necessary first step for many people in demonstrating a higher level of respect for others. However, I feel the word 'tolerance' does not adequately illustrate, promote, or require an actual change in belief or attitude. A term that I believe actually encourages and inspires true change is "Acceptance". 'Acceptance' demonstrates a genuine and definitive alteration in our perception and beliefs. The decision in how we see and perceive others is entirely up to us to decide, and begins with how and what we are taught. What we universally demonstrate through our actions and how we communicate with our children is an extremely important part in how we perceive and accept each other. It is through the eyes and minds of our children that universal acceptance can be achieved for them, and generations to come.

The true foundation for "Acceptance" is, 'understanding'. As you read the text, you'll notice that it starts out simple and basic in its description of how we are all different. The initial focus is on colors and how they relate to our physical being. This makes it easy for a child to understand and relate to color being a very common characteristic of who we all are. The illustrations can also be utilized as a teaching method to learn colors as they associate them with facial characteristics. The illustrations are all on the right-hand page with the accompanying verse on the left. If the child sits to the right of the reader, not only can they touch and point out the people and characteristics in the illustrations, they can also play an active role in the reading of the book by being the page turner. The text gradually matures in its content and message, so as the child matures, it can be read again at various points of the child's development to reveal a deeper meaning and a broader understanding. The maturation of the text also promotes communication between the reader and the child as it will undoubtedly generate questions from the child regarding some of the meaning of the text, as well as to the significance of the illustrations.   As a result, the reader becomes more than just the narrator. He or she becomes the messenger of the meaning of the text by using their own words, which in the child's mind, secures the credibility of the message in each verse.

Another communication opportunity, as well as a method for building the child's perception, is to play 'Find the Differences' between the first illustration of the WE sculpture on the hill that corresponds with the first verse, and the one that corresponds to the last verse. The most obvious is the presence and then the absence of the ME shadow, which is symbolic of the acceptance of WE. Other differences are characters changing places, new ones added, addition of a pair of sunglasses, and a different dog. See how many you can find!

Lastly, but certainly no less important, is the positive impact I hope "WE" will have upon the person reading this book to a child, whether they are a senior, an adult, a teen, or an adolescent. It is my sincere hope that for those who may have their own negative viewpoints and perceptions of others that are based solely on the universal characteristics of race, color, gender, physical characteristics, physical and/or mental limitations, or chosen personal relationships, that they are inspired to reconsider their views after reading "WE".

Thank you very much,
William R. Mrazek

Have you noticed that there appears to be,

many more people than just you and me?

Some are narrow,

some are **wide**,

some may be in the middle.

Some are young,

some are OLD;

for others, age is a RIDDLE.

Some are short,

some are tall,

some are in-between.

Eyes are BLUE,

eyes are BROWN,

maybe even GREEN.

BLUE

BROWN

GREEN

Hair can be yellow, brown, black,

or red; even gray or white.

Some people have no hair at all,

there is no wrong or right.

Our faces are all different;

in **size**, and *shape*, and color, too.

If we all looked the same,

we'd wonder;

"Is that them,

or me,

or you?"

Color is the reason why,

there is more than black and white.

But we need to see with our minds,

as well as with our sight.

People may walk, at times they run,

some use a special chair.

It doesn't matter how they go,

to get from here to there.

Some people wear clothes

we may not choose;

making fun is not a game.

No one would listen to music,

if the songs all sounded the same.

This music all
sounds the same. How boring!

Voices may sound different,

with words you don't understand.

People come from other places,

other homes, or distant lands.

Hawaii, United States
English
"WE" is pronounced "We"

Quebec, Canada
French
"WE" is pronounced "Nous"

Moscow, Russia
Russian
"WE" is pronounced "Mi"

Peru, South America
Spanish
"WE" is pronounced "Nosotros"

Namibia (Herero), Africa
Otjiherero
"WE" is pronounced "Eṱe"

Beijing, China
Mandarin
"WE" is pronounced "Wo Men"

You can never have too many friends,

I know this to be true.

But do not judge by how they look,

but by what they say and do.

Everyone is different;

   it's the one thing that we all share.

Accepting we are not the same,

   is a better way to care.

There's one more important thing to know,

before this book is through;

everyone needs both love and respect,

as much as me and you.

So now you see there

are many more people,

than just you and me.

There is a special word for all of us;

that special word is "We".

CPSIA information can be obtained at www.ICGtesting.com
Printed in the USA
LVIW01n2348210217
525012LV00007B/23